THE YEAR END REFLECTION
GUIDE

A WRITE YOUR WAY JOURNALING BONUS

THE JOURNALING MASTERY SERIES: THEORY
AND PRACTICE
BOOK 3

RICHARD FRENCH

Indie Pen Press

TURNING DREAMS INTO BESTSELLERS

Indie Pen Press
Gig Harbor WA 98332
IndiePenPress.com

First Edition December 2024

Paperback ISBN: 979-8-9917570-7-2

✳ Created with Vellum

ONE
THE POWER OF SYSTEMATIC
REFLECTION

S arah sat at her desk, surrounded by a year's worth of journals. Outside, snow fell softly in the December twilight, but her attention was fixed on the volumes before her —each containing months of experiences, insights, and growth waiting to be understood. She'd been here before, at previous year's ends, always intending to make sense of it all but feeling overwhelmed by the sheer volume of life captured in these pages.

"There has to be a better way," she whispered, running her fingers along the spine of her latest journal. She'd written faithfully throughout the year, processing daily experiences, tracking goals, and exploring ideas. But now, facing the task of understanding it all, she felt lost. Where should she begin? How could she transform these scattered insights into mean-ingful guidance for the year ahead?

Sarah's situation mirrors that of many journal keepers as the year draws to a close. We write regularly, collecting moments and memories, insights, and ideas. But when it comes time to step back and make sense of it all, we often find ourselves over-whelmed. Random review—flipping through pages hoping for insight—rarely reveals the deeper patterns and profound lessons hidden within our experiences.

This is where systematic reflection becomes crucial. Just as scientists wouldn't analyze data by casually glancing at their notes, we shouldn't approach our year-end reflection without a proper framework. The stories of our lives deserve careful, intentional review.

As Sarah was about to discover, transforming overwhelming information into clear insight isn't about reading more—it's about reading differently. It's about having a system that helps you not just remember your experiences but understand them. A framework that reveals not just what happened but what it means for your journey ahead.

In the following pages, you'll discover a structured approach to year-end reflection that transforms overwhelming information into clear guidance for your future. You'll learn how to extract meaningful patterns from your experiences, understand the more profound significance of your challenges and victories, and create actionable insights for the year ahead.

This isn't just another review process. It's a systematic approach to understanding your year's journey—one that honors your experiences and future potential. Whether you're a seasoned journal keeper or just beginning to document your journey, this guide will help you transform your year's writings into wisdom that guides your path forward.

Let's begin this journey of discovery together, starting with understanding why systematic reflection matters and how it differs from casual review.

TWO
UNDERSTANDING SYSTEMATIC YEAR-END REFLECTION

The difference between random review and systematic reflection mirrors the difference between looking at a puzzle's pieces and actually assembling them into a complete picture. Many of us approach year-end reflections like rummaging through a box of memories—pulling out whatever catches our attention, briefly considering it, and then moving on. While this might surface occasional insights, it misses the deeper patterns that make our experiences meaningful.

Let me share a story that illustrates this difference. Michael, a business leader I worked with, had kept detailed journals for years. Each December, he'd spend a weekend reading through them, noting what stood out. "I always felt like I was missing something," he told me. "I'd find interesting moments, but I couldn't see how they connected or what they meant for my future."

Then Michael learned about systematic reflection. Instead of random review, he began using a structured approach that helped him see patterns, understand connections, and extract meaningful insights from his experiences. "It was like putting on glasses for the first time," he explained. "Suddenly, I could see how different parts of my year connected. Challenges that seemed random showed clear patterns. Successes I'd over-looked revealed important lessons."

THE CORE ELEMENTS OF SYSTEMATIC REFLECTION

Systematic reflection differs from random review in several crucial ways:

1. **Intentional Structure** Instead of letting your attention wander, systematic reflection guides you through specific aspects of your experience. Like a skilled interviewer, it asks the right questions in the proper order, helping you uncover more profound insights.

2. **Pattern Recognition** Rather than viewing experiences in isolation, systematic reflection helps you identify connections and themes. It reveals how different parts of your life influence each other and how patterns develop over time.

3. **Progressive Depth** Like peeling an onion, systematic reflection takes you through layers of understanding. Each phase builds on the previous one, helping you move from surface observations to deeper insights.

4. **Integration Focus:** Instead of simply remembering what happened, systematic reflection helps you understand what your experiences mean and how to use these insights moving forward.

CREATING YOUR REFLECTION SPACE

Before we discuss the specific framework, let's consider setting up for success. Effective reflection requires both physical and mental space.

Physical Space

Find a quiet location where you won't be interrupted. Gather your materials:

- Your journals from the past year
- A fresh notebook for insights
- Your favorite pen
- Any additional materials that help you think clearly (calendar, planning documents, etc.)
- Something to drink (water, tea, coffee)

Consider the environment. Good lighting, comfortable seating, and adequate space to spread your materials all matter. Some people find that background music helps them focus, while others prefer silence.

Mental Space

Equally important is preparing your mind for reflection:

- Choose a time when you're mentally fresh
- Clear pending tasks that might distract you
- Set clear boundaries with others about your reflection time
- Release expectations about what you "should" discover
- Approach with curiosity rather than judgment

THE TIME INVESTMENT

One common mistake is trying to complete year-end reflection in a single session. This often leads to surface-level insights and mental fatigue. Instead, I recommend spreading your reflection over several sessions:

- Initial Review: 2-3 hours
- Pattern Recognition: 1-2 hours
- Deep Analysis: 2-3 hours
- Integration and Planning: 1-2 hours

These sessions can be spread across days or weeks, allowing insights to develop and deeper patterns to emerge. Remember, we're not just collecting memories—we're developing an understanding that will guide our future.

COMMON PITFALLS TO AVOID

Before we move into the specific framework, let's address some common pitfalls:

1. **The Highlight Reel Trap:** Don't focus only on major events. Often, the most significant insights come from subtle patterns in daily life.
2. **The Negativity Bias** Many people naturally focus on challenges and difficulties. Remember to give equal attention to successes and positive patterns.
3. **The Resolution Rush** Avoid jumping straight to planning for the future before fully understanding the lessons of the past year.
4. **The Comparison Trap:** Your journey is unique. Resist

the urge to compare your experiences with others' highlight reels.

5. **The Perfect Memory Myth:** You don't need to remember everything. The framework will help you identify what's most significant for your growth.

As we dive into the Five-Phase Reflection Framework, remember that this process isn't about judgment. It's about understanding—understanding that transforms experience into wisdom and wisdom into positive change.

In the next chapter, we'll explore each phase of the framework in detail, starting with the Memory Sweep that helps you gather the raw material for deeper reflection.

THREE
THE FIVE-PHASE REFLECTION FRAMEWORK

As Emma spread her journals across her desk, color-coded tabs marking significant moments, she remembered how differently she'd approached year-end reflection in the past. "I used to flip through pages randomly," she told me, "hoping for insights to jump out. Now I understand that meaningful reflection, like any important process, needs a framework."

The Five-Phase Reflection Framework transforms overwhelming information into clear insight systematically. Each phase builds upon the previous one, creating a deeper understanding of your year's journey.

PHASE 1: THE MEMORY SWEEP

Think of the Memory Sweep as creating a map of your year's territory. We're not analyzing yet—simply gathering information in a structured way.

The Month-by-Month Process

Start with January and work forward, using these Memory Activation Prompts for each month:

1. Setting the Scene

- Where were you physically during this month?
- What was your primary focus or goal?
- What was your emotional state?

2. Key Events

- What significant events occurred?
- What decisions did you make?
- What changes took place?

3. Daily Patterns

- What occupied most of your time?
- Who were the key people in your life?
- What habits were you practicing?

Emma's Example: "Reviewing March, I noticed I was primarily working from home, focused on launching our new project. I felt anxious but excited. The significant event was presented to the board, but equally important was the daily pattern of early morning meditation I'd started. Looking at it systematically showed me how my morning practice helped me handle the presentation stress—a connection I'd previously missed."

Creating Your Timeline

As you work through each month, create a simple timeline. Note:

- Major events
- Key decisions
- Significant changes
- Pattern shifts
- Important conversations

Don't worry about analysis yet—just create a clear picture of what happened when.

PHASE 2: PATTERN RECOGNITION

Now that we have our map, we can start identifying patterns. This phase reveals the themes and cycles that shaped your year.

Types of Patterns to Look For:

1. Emotional Patterns

- What emotions appeared regularly?
- What triggered them?
- How did they influence your decisions?

2. Behavioral Patterns

- What actions did you repeat?
- Which habits strengthened or weakened?
- How did your routines evolve?

3. Relationship Patterns

- Who consistently appeared in your story?
- How did relationships change?
- What patterns emerged in your interactions?

4. Growth Patterns

- Where did you see progress?
- What challenges repeated?
- How did your responses evolve?

Practice Example: "Looking at my year, I noticed that major breakthroughs often followed periods of doubt and confusion. This pattern repeated in March with the project launch, in July with my role transition, and in October with the team restructure. Understanding this helped me see that periods of uncertainty weren't failures—they were often preludes to growth."

PHASE 3: IMPACT ANALYSIS

In this phase, we examine the consequences and ripple effects of our experiences and choices.

Areas to Analyze:

1. Decision Impact

- What were the results of key decisions?
- How did they affect different life areas?
- What unexpected consequences emerged?

2. Growth Measurement

- How did you progress toward your goals?
- What unplanned growth occurred?
- Where did you face resistance?

3. Relationship Effects

- How did your choices affect others?
- How did others' choices affect you?
- What relationship dynamics shifted?

4. Environmental Influence

- How did external circumstances affect you?
- How did you adapt to changes?
- What resources proved most valuable?

PHASE 4: WISDOM INTEGRATION

This phase transforms observations into understanding and insights into principles.

Key Activities:

1. Lesson Extraction

- What did each major experience teach you?
- What wisdom emerged from challenges?
- What successes revealed about your strengths?

2. Principle Development

- What truths became clear this year?
- What beliefs were challenged or confirmed?
- What new understanding emerged?

3. Strategy Recognition

- What approaches worked well?
- What methods proved ineffective?
- What new strategies did you develop?

Integration Example: "Through this analysis, I realized that my best work happened when I combined structured planning with creative exploration. This became a new principle: 'Create frameworks that enable freedom.' This insight now guides how I approach both professional projects and personal goals."

PHASE 5: FUTURE INTEGRATION

The final phase bridges past insights with future intentions.

Creating Forward Movement:

1. Pattern Projection

- Which patterns serve your growth?
- Which patterns need modification?
- What new patterns want to emerge?

2. Intention Setting

- What insights guide your next steps?
- What experiments want to unfold?
- What commitments feel aligned?

3. Implementation Planning

- How will you apply your learnings?
- What support structures need to be in place?
- How will you track progress?

Remember, this framework isn't rigid—it's a guide that helps ensure you don't miss important aspects of your reflection. Move through it at your own pace, trusting that each phase builds upon the previous ones to create a complete under-standing of your year's journey.

FOUR
MAKING IT WORK - PRACTICAL APPLICATION

The framework is powerful, but like any tool, its value lies in how you use it. Let me share how Rachel, a creative director and mother of two, adapted the system to her real-world constraints and challenges.

"I couldn't set aside whole days for reflection," Rachel explained. "Instead, I broke it down into manageable pieces and created a process that worked with my life, not against it."

TIME MANAGEMENT STRATEGIES

The 30-Minute Method

Rather than trying to find large blocks of time, Rachel used focused 30-minute sessions:

1. Morning Sessions (6:30-7:00 AM)

- Perfect for Memory Sweep
- Mind is fresh

- House is quiet
- Focus on one month per session

2. Lunch Break Reviews (12:30-1:00 PM)

- Ideal for Pattern Recognition
- Natural pause in the day
- Can be done while eating
- Easy to maintain momentum

3. Evening Integration (9:00-9:30 PM)

- Best for Wisdom Integration
- Day's tasks are complete
- Reflective mindset
- Can connect to regular journaling

Remember: Consistent small sessions often prove more effective than irregular long ones.

OVERCOMING COMMON OBSTACLES

1. The Overwhelm Response

When facing a year's worth of experiences, it's natural to feel overwhelmed. Try these approaches:

- Start with the most recent month
- Focus on one area of life at a time
- Use the checklist method (√ each completed review)
- Celebrate small completions

2. Missing Documentation

What if you didn't journal consistently? Look for alternative memory anchors:

- Calendar entries
- Photos on your phone
- Email archives
- Social media posts
- Project milestones
- Bank statements (they tell a story of priorities)

3. Emotional Resistance

Sometimes we avoid reflection because we're not ready to face certain experiences:

- Start with neutral or positive memories
- Use the "Observer Perspective" technique
- Set emotional boundaries ("I'll look at this for 10 minutes")
- Have support available if needed
- Remember: Understanding differs from dwelling

MAINTAINING MOMENTUM

Keep your reflection practice moving forward with these strategies:

1. The Progress Map

Create a visual representation of your review progress:

- Calendar with completed phases marked
- Checklist of reviewed months
- Pattern collection growing

- Insights gathered

2. The Insight Tracker

Maintain an "Insights Page" where you list key discoveries:

- Patterns noticed
- Lessons learned
- Questions emerging
- Themes developing

3. The Integration Bridge

Connect your reflection practice to daily life:

- Morning preview of recent insights
- Midday check-in with patterns
- Evening connection to current experiences

SPECIAL CIRCUMSTANCES

Handling Difficult Years

Some years contain experiences we'd rather not revisit. approach these with care:

1. Set Clear Boundaries

- Decide what you're ready to examine
- Know your emotional limits
- Have support available
- Take breaks when needed

2. Use the Container Method

- Mentally "contain" difficult experiences
- Set specific times to process them
- Return to safer territory as needed
- Celebrate your courage in looking

Processing Success and Growth

Surprisingly, some find it challenging to fully acknowledge their successes:

1. The Success Inventory

- List all achievements, large and small
- Note progress in different areas
- Include "invisible" growth
- Celebrate unexpected wins

2. The Growth Grid

- Map skills developed
- Track challenges overcome
- Note new capabilities
- Document expanded comfort zones

INTEGRATION WITH REGULAR PRACTICE

Your year-end reflection should connect naturally with your ongoing journaling:

1. Creating Context

- Note patterns you're watching for
- Tag entries related to identified themes
- Track progress on insights gained

- Document new understanding as it emerges

2. Monthly Mini-Reviews

- Schedule brief monthly check-ins
- Review patterns in progress
- Update your insight tracker
- Adjust course as needed

3. Quarterly Connections

- Deeper pattern review every three months
- Check progress on identified areas
- Update your growth map
- Refine your approach as needed

Remember, the goal isn't perfect implementation—it's consistent progress toward deeper understanding. Let your practice evolve as you learn what works best for you.

FIVE
SPECIAL CONSIDERATIONS

Life isn't always a straight line of progress and achievement. Some years bring unexpected challenges, profound losses, or periods of significant transition. This chapter addresses how to adapt your reflection practice to honor these complex experiences.

HANDLING CHALLENGING YEARS

David sat with his journal, pen hovering over the page. "How do I reflect on a year that included both my divorce and my mother's passing?" he asked during one of our sessions. His question touches on a crucial aspect of systematic reflection: honoring difficulty while finding growth.

The Compassionate Review Method

1. Create Safe Entry Points

- Begin with neutral territory
- Acknowledge difficult periods without diving in

- Map the landscape before exploring details
- Set clear boundaries for exploration

2. Use the Spiral Approach

- Start at the edges of challenging experiences
- Gradually move closer to core events
- Return to safe ground when needed
- Honor your own timing

David's Example: "I started by reviewing my work projects from that period. This gave me solid ground to stand on before looking at the personal challenges. I discovered that my professional resilience actually grew during this time—an insight I might have missed with a less structured approach."

PROCESSING GRIEF AND LOSS

When reflection includes periods of loss, consider these approaches:

1. The Memory Container Practice

- Create specific time boundaries for reviewing difficult memories
- Use physical objects (like a special candle) to mark reflection time
- Have clear opening and closing rituals
- Know your support resources

2. The Growth Within Grief Framework

- Acknowledge both the loss and the learning

- Notice unexpected sources of support
- Recognize newly developed strengths
- Honor changes in perspective

3. The Legacy Integration Process

- Consider what the experience taught you
- Note how it changed your priorities
- Recognize new wisdom gained
- Honor how it shaped your path

CELEBRATING UNEXPECTED WINS

Sometimes the most significant growth comes disguised as setbacks. Lisa discovered this while reviewing what she'd initially considered a "lost year":

"What looked like career failure—losing my corporate job—actually launched my own consulting business. The systematic review helped me see how that 'setback' freed me to pursue what I really wanted."

The Hidden Victory Inventory

1. Direct Victories

- Expected achievements
- Planned progress
- Clear successes

2. Indirect Victories

- Growth through challenges
- Unexpected opportunities

- Strength discovered in difficulty

3. Character Victories

- Enhanced resilience
- Deepened wisdom
- Expanded capacity

BALANCING PERSONAL AND PROFESSIONAL REFLECTION

Many find their personal and professional lives deeply inter-twined. Here's how to honor both domains:

The Integration Map

1. Identify Overlapping Themes

- How personal growth affects professional performance
- How professional challenges impact personal life
- Where boundaries need strengthening
- Where integration creates synergy

2. Track Parallel Development

- Professional skills enhancing personal life
- Personal growth supporting career advancement
- Relationship skills improving both domains
- Leadership emerging in multiple areas

The Balance Sheet Method

Create parallel columns to examine:

- Professional achievements | Personal growth
- Career challenges | Life lessons
- Work relationships | Personal connections
- Professional goals | Personal aspirations

INCLUDING OTHERS IN YOUR REFLECTION

While reflection is primarily personal, sometimes including others enriches the process:

1. The Shared Perspective Approach

- Invite trusted friends to share their observations
- Compare perspectives on shared experiences
- Gather feedback on observed growth
- Create dialogue around common challenges

2. The Relationship Review

- Examine how key relationships evolved
- Notice patterns in connections
- Identify relationship lessons
- Plan relationship growth

3. The Community Impact Assessment

- Consider your influence on others
- Notice ripple effects of your choices
- Recognize collective growth
- Honor shared achievements

CREATING SACRED SPACE

Regardless of what your year contained, create space that honors the significance of your reflection:

Physical Space

- Choose a location that supports introspection
- Remove distractions
- Include meaningful objects
- Consider comfort and practicality

Temporal Space

- Set aside dedicated time
- Create clear boundaries
- Honor your reflection schedule
- Allow for organic timing

Emotional Space

- Acknowledge all feelings
- Release judgment
- Welcome insights
- Trust the process

Remember: Every experience, whether challenging or celebratory, contains seeds of wisdom. Systematic reflection helps us find and nurture these seeds, allowing them to grow into deeper understanding and purposeful action.

SIX

MOVING FORWARD

As the sun rose over the city, Sarah returned to her desk, her year-end reflection nearly complete. The scattered journals that had once overwhelmed her now told a coherent story of growth, challenge, and transformation. But the real question remained: How would she turn these insights into positive change?

CREATING YOUR REFLECTION SCHEDULE

The power of systematic reflection lies not just in the year-end process, but in how it informs your path forward. Let's establish a structure that helps you maintain momentum and build on your insights.

The Three-Tier Review System

1. Monthly Check-ins (2-3 hours)

- Review the month's experiences
- Track identified patterns

- Update your insight collection
- Adjust course as needed

2. Quarterly Deep Dives (4-6 hours)

- Comprehensive pattern review
- Progress assessment
- Strategy refinement
- Forward planning

3. Annual Reflection (8-12 hours spread over time)

- Complete system implementation
- Full pattern analysis
- Comprehensive integration
- Vision development

Emma's Example: "I schedule my monthly reviews for the first Sunday of each month, quarterly reviews align with the seasons, and I start my annual reflection in early December. This rhythm keeps me connected to my insights while building toward deeper understanding."

SETTING UP ACCOUNTABILITY

Maintaining a reflection practice requires support. Consider these approaches:

1. Personal Accountability

- Calendar all review sessions in advance
- Set clear completion criteria
- Track your reflection practice

- Celebrate consistency

2. Partner Accountability

- Find a reflection buddy
- Schedule check-in sessions
- Share insights (as appropriate)
- Support each other's practice

3. Community Accountability

- Join a journaling group
- Share your commitment
- Participate in discussions
- Contribute to collective learning

MAINTAINING PERSPECTIVE

As you move forward, remember these key principles:

The Growth Spiral

Understanding isn't linear—it spirals upward, often returning to similar themes at deeper levels. This means:

- Previous insights may need revisiting
- Old patterns might need reexamination
- Earlier understanding might deepen
- New perspectives can emerge on familiar territory

The Integration Timeline

True integration takes time. Allow your insights to:

- Settle into awareness
- Inform daily choices
- Shape new patterns
- Guide future reflection

The Wisdom Bridge

Your reflections create a bridge between:

- Past experience and future choice
- Understanding and action
- Insight and implementation
- Personal growth and practical change

CONNECTING TO YOUR LARGER LIFE STORY

Your year-end reflection fits within a larger narrative:

1. Story Integration

- How does this year connect to your larger journey?
- What themes are continuing?
- What new chapters are beginning?
- What story wants to unfold?

2. Vision Alignment

- How do your insights inform your future?
- What possibilities are emerging?
- What directions call to you?
- What wants to grow through you?

3. Legacy Consideration

- What wisdom are you gathering?
- What patterns serve your purpose?
- What contributions are emerging?
- What gifts are you developing?

BUILDING ON YOUR INSIGHTS

Transform your understanding into action:

1. Create Implementation Plans

- Identify key areas for change
- Set clear, achievable goals
- Establish support systems
- Schedule regular reviews

2. Design Growth Experiments

- Test new approaches
- Try different strategies
- Explore emerging interests
- Develop new capabilities

3. Cultivate Supportive Habits

- Morning reflection time
- Regular journaling practice
- Consistent review sessions
- Ongoing learning

THE JOURNEY CONTINUES

Remember, systematic reflection isn't about perfect implementation—it's about consistent growth and deepening
understanding. As you move forward:

- Trust the process
- Honor your timing
- Welcome insights
- Celebrate progress
- Stay curious
- Keep exploring

Your journey of reflection and growth continues, one insight,
one pattern, one understanding at a time. Each reflection
builds upon the last, creating a rich tapestry of wisdom that
informs and enriches your path forward.

As you close this guide and return to your journals, remember:
The patterns you've discovered, the insights you've gained,
and the wisdom you've gathered are not just memories of what
was—they are seeds of what can be. Tend them well, and
watch how they grow.

Made in the USA
Columbia, SC
09 November 2024

45821839R00022